Moonlight Storms and Sunshine

ISBN-13: 9798615426209

Thank you:

I want to thank my husband, Francesco (Seco) for pushing me and not letting me put this book on the back burner, or letting it fade into non-existence. Your support and love is incredible. You are my rock. I love you.

Thank you to my mom for being my superwoman, to all those nights as a child you would come to my rescue, I know I can always call on you. You are such an amazing woman. I love you mama.

Thank you to my dad for all you have done for me. We may have had a rocky start, but I couldn't be happier and feel more blessed with how our relationship has evolved. I love you.

Most importantly, I must thank God.

before we begin, I want to make a note. I have poems in here about my dad, but I want to point out that these poems are written in past tense. Amazingly, my dad has been sober for a few years now, and I am so incredibly proud of him. Our relationship has transformed, and I love where it has evolved to. But, I still wanted to acknowledge the past, especially if it can help you.

Her mind is like moonlight storms
and sunshine.
it can be dark, and scary
yet at the same time produce light.
--she has a mental disorder.

Innocence always leaves
before its ready to.

God has given us a voice,
not to be silent
but to shout to the treetops and above
that you need help.

   --It's okay to need help, and it's okay to shout it.

Her innocence was wrapped up
in the loss of innocence.

You pick at your fingernails
and bounce your legs up and down
while sitting at the edge of your bed
not sure of what just happened to you.
you're scared,
and want to escape and run from yourself.
but realize no matter how fast you go
your shadow can keep up.
you have been given scars that should have never
belonged to you
or found residence on your body.
and I know you feel trapped,
under an authority that doesn't recognize
the innocence in your eyes
as they violate you
and steal from you.
but my love,
this is not the end.
this will not be the end.
you will get out.
you will be set free from hands
that were never meant to touch you.
use your voice.

Shall I compare thee to a summer's day?
maybe not…
you were more like a cold winter's night
bitter and stiff like ice.
you didn't leave room for warmth
and even if you did
it only lasted for a moment.
for even in winter,
the sun shined
but its warmth
had trouble reaching you.

She walks hallways
where storms rise
where thunder pounds
and lightning cracks above her head
the storms follow her and won't ease up
and she hasn't done anything to cause them
just existed.
-to her, someone being bullied.

He holds his head at attention,
he has achieved something all young boys fantasize
about.
he whispered in all his friends' ears of what he has
done and
pounds his fists in the air.
he penetrated through hearts
to reach last base.
and slide into home plate
with nothing but a trophy to place on his shelf.
while she lays in pain
alone
and confused.

Your home holds onto late night arguments
and midnight fights
your room is your safe place,
no one and nothing
can reach you there.
you hide under your blankets
and cover your ears
yet sound still has a great way
of sneaking and squeezing through spaces.
so muffled shouts rock you to sleep.

She is superwoman
wrapped in a warm embrace
she holds you tight
and places her hand on your chest
to remind you to breathe
she feels your pulse at the base of your wrist
and reassures you
that you are alive.
she promises it will all be over soon
as she holds your scared and shaking body.
she is wonder woman
the strongest woman alive.
she places herself in front of bullets
so you never get hit
she stood in front of storms
so you couldn't feel its winds
she is also superman
as she stood in places where superman
should have
but never did.
--she is my mommy.

You've gone down roads
that didn't welcome you
and you've walked paths
that didn't want you.
yet, you continued to walk.
don't blame yourself,
you were led by those you trusted,
and just like before, they proved
untrustworthy.

In the autumn
the leaves change colors.
it is not something they plan
they just do.
they know when the crisp air hits their veins
and whispers a cool breeze down their spine
it is time to die.
time to show the world its beauty
before winter takes over
it's one of our last reminders
before the year ends
that change can be powerful
and that just like the leaves
dying to your old self
is necessary if you
want to be created anew.

She wonders if her body is all
she has to offer
if that's all any man wants.
she has given it away too many times
and wished she could take it all back.
one by one
the pieces of her
are scattered about
here and there.
she looks around to steal herself back
but they hold her under
lock and key.
but she is ready to break in
and take back what belongs to
her.

She wanders the aisles looking for the heart
she lost.
not remembering it was long gone;
driving down the road full of adventures
searching for its long-lost owner
who left it with a stranger.
-don't go home with him, I.

The snow has turned your hands bright red
but, you can't go inside.
you can't face what lies between you and the door.
so you run.
in the dead of winter you run.
you're not sure where,
but anywhere is better than there.
snow rests in your hair,
and builds up on your shoulders,
but you have decided to continue on.
i understand you had to leave;
before the demons who live within the walls of your home
had another chance to prey on you.
but please, go somewhere safe.
don't wander the streets tonight.
don't stay out too dark.
because that's when the wolves come out to play
and when a predator recognizes a wounded baby they charge.
--there is always someone willing to help. (a best friend, a family member, the police)

Her mind has a way of playing
mind games with her.
a twisted sense of humor
that she is tired of.
-anxiety, I.

When will the day come when dreams
equal reality,
and reality is actually real
and not a dream?

She breathes in midnight air
gasping for the stars
she suffocates on darkness
as she walks with her head down
a block away from his bed.
she inhales the nighttime coolness
and exhales the remanence of him.
she wants to forget
what happened under the moonlight
before the storm arrives in the morning.
- don't go home with him, II.

Beautiful is the life that is lived.
the life that tries again
and again.
the one that gives tomorrows a chance.
beautiful is the life that pushed through today
to stay until tomorrow.
you are the beautiful life.
stay until there are no more tomorrows
which means never leave.
-stay, I.

-An Ode to mental health-
she is daytime sunshine
and morning moon shows.
she is also clear skied rainstorms
and the eye of a hurricane.
while at the same time,
a category eight storm.
-she is me…unpredictable, yet at the same time
predictable.

There are dreams left undreamed
sunrises left unseen
there are kisses, un-kissed
and hugs never gotten.
there are storms never conquered
and beautiful days never lived
before you decide to leave me here tonight
remember why you've been
fighting to live.
-stay, II.

Have you ever wondering
why silence is so loud
and why whispers share all secrets
and how many promises seem to be broken?
-i'm still searching for this answer, but I think it lies
within the heart of mankind.

She is moon and stars
and sometimes sun.
when she rains she pours
and when she shines
she shimmers.
she feels too much
or maybe not enough
but she remains steady in the wind
for although she is broken,
she is solid.
-so are you.

She hears whispers in the dark
and she listens
but the whispers she thought
she could trust,
she couldn't.
-don't listen.

Pain finds a resting place
deep within your heart.
you press it down
beneath your bones;
so the only way to find
the pain
is to break you.
-it's okay to be broken.

Since when has nightmares
taken place in beautiful dreams?
-anxiety, II.

She covers her face in shame
while exiting a room she never knew.
she wipes away a lonely tear
and drops her eyes to the ground.
she can't remember her steps
or what led her there.
but under the new day's morning sun
she wanders until she finds home again.
-don't go home with him, III.

You're afraid to live any longer and
death seems to be your only option.
but what if I tell you,
you can change your life into anything you want?
would you stay then?
it's never impossible to change your circumstances.
-stay, III.

I know these words may not be enough.
but I pray that they
wrap around you
and give you the strength
to keep living to see tomorrow.
i wrote these words just for you.
-stay, IV.

Hold these words in your heart
keep them close to you,
and anytime you feel like it's the end
read them and remember it doesn't have
to end
this way.
tomorrow needs to see you
tomorrow wants to see you smile
and
so do I.
-Send me a picture of you tomorrow, smiling.-
--stay, IV.

If I ever run out of ideas to write,
like now,
i will babble until words form on the page,
and I filter out the bad,
to get to the good.
just like you must filter out the bad
to once again see happy days.

You will find me
covered in moonlight
littered with stars in
my eyes
among the forest walls,
where owls sing their
midnight song
and sleep fills the
autumn nights air.
i'm the girl dancing to
the wind
and swaying to the
sound of water
streaming by.
i imagine a life with no
fear
no racing heart
or nightmared thoughts
that echo in caves
that normally pull me
in.
these thoughts.
these thoughts,
they have a way of
speaking to me
they take me by my
hand
and lead me down a
path of darkness
they want me to get
lost
so they release my
hand
and leave me trapped
in
the blackened labyrinth
that is my own mind.
but not tonight.
tonight I will continue
my dance in moonlight
accompanied by
swaying trees
i will catch shooting
stars
and place them
amongst my eyes
and sing with the owls
the gentle sounds of
night,
because tonight,
these thoughts cannot
haunt me
for I have locked them
away
in the hands of God
and in order to escape,
they have to go
through, Him.

so dance with me the
dance of freedom.
for most nightmares
comes at night,
but tonight,
i'm carefree,

swaying to the song of
liberty.
-goodbye, anxiety I.

You can find me sitting on the clouds
drifting through the air
watching the world below me.
you can find me on treetops
swaying with the leaves
enjoying the breeze
you can find me in the water
floating downstream
to the sounds of fish swimming by.
you can find me
under moonlight
sitting with the owls
unafraid of the dark
you can find me on my knees
praying to a God
who speaks back to me.
and He'll speak back to you, too
-goodbye anxiety, II.

I walk amongst the midnight hour
and hold hands with stars
i'm not afraid of the dark
for I have a light inside of me.
-thank you Lord.

A single thought stirs up
the demons inside my head
my breathing stops
and my heart beat fills my body
i can feel it in my feet
yet I feel no blood pumping
to my brain
i feel lightheaded
as if I'm going to faint right here
right now
i try to breathe
yet oxygen bypasses my lungs
i roll my window down
and let the sharp cold wind
hit my face
is this when I crash
i think to myself
my breathing fluctuates
and I fight to reach my destination
i'm alive
i need to breathe
i'm alive
i feel my heartbeat
i begin to relax
yet it takes hours
for me to get my breath back to normal
as I pull into the Target parking lot.
-anxiety happens anywhere, at any time.

You've been holding onto too much
you've been living each day
trying to forget what has happened to you
but this weight is too much too bare
your body holds onto it all
but you don't have to hold it any longer.
you must acknowledge it
you must let it go.
or else,
you will drown by this extra weight
you will sink
so deep
a rescue will be nearly impossible.
you won't float
you'll sink
so let's work through this,
together.
through these words
in this here book.
Let's lighten your load
within the lines of these poems.

It's clear skies today
but a storm comes
tomorrow.
it's raining out now
but the sun is to come
out in an hour.
the snow is falling hard
yet, it melts shortly after.
waves are crashing
yet in a moments time
the seas will lay still.
my mind is like the weather.
every minute can bring
something different,
without warning
with no time to prepare.

The fog comes and I can't see.
it clouds my vision
like thick smoke
it burns my eyes
and makes it hard
to breathe
hard to think
hard to stay standing
up right.
this fog covers
and lays over so much of my brain
that it's hard to find
my common sense
amidst the smoke
of fear, anxiety,
and OCD.

When was the last time
you thanked God
for the things you
went through?
yeah, it hurts.
yes, it was tragic.
but there was and
is a reason.
maybe, it's time to talk
to God to figure it out.
fire purifies many things
so, yes, you stood in the fire
and got burned
but even
silver and gold
nccd to adhere to extreme heat
to shine.
thank God for you battles
because without them
where would you be
what wouldn't you have learned
who would you be now,
and now ask yourself,
who can you help?
-God doesn't give us more than we can handle,
and He gives us everything for a reason.

Is there darkness over you tonight?
are your thoughts whispering to you
are your tears calling out
to you in this moment?
they're asking for you to follow them
but you must go the other direction
go down the other path
ignore their calls
their chants
and their pleas for help.
it's a trap.
they don't need you.
they know what to say to draw you in.
so, be brave
the path that seems dark is not
there is a light that will guide you
down the opposite path
where voices of demons don't reside
but only the voice of God.
-follow God's voice.

She wanders down paths she doesn't know.
they change with each walk,
and the ending destination
is new each time.
she wonders the bedrooms
of men she doesn't know
to fill an emptiness deep inside that
no man,
no person,
can fill.
this hole that lays hallow,
can only be filled by God,
and it remains
in His absence.
call Him back, for He never left you,
you just didn't realize He was there.
-don't go home with him, IV.

It all started with a lonely heart
mixed with the deep desire to be loved.
it's this combo at such a young age
that can lead to many mistakes.

She was taught by those around her
that being sexual meant you
will get love.
but, I look now at all the unloved, sexy girls
in the world
and wonder
when did that lie start.

There are times I think back to
my younger self
and hold my head in shame
i want to look in the mirror
and see myself 14 again
and warn her of the dangers that lie ahead
i want to look her in the eyes
and tell her
no matter how hard I look
a dad's love will not be found
in boys who only want one thing you're offering,
and it's not your heart.

Your deep unhappiness
that keeps you awake
began much earlier in
your life than you think.
time to take a trip
down memory lane
and get to the bottom of your broken heart.

I know you want to end it here
and now.
you believe your midnight cries have gone unheard,
but,
i hear them
and I'm talking to you
here and now
through these very pages.
don't end it now,
give yourself another day
and another after that,
and another after that
and as many others after that,
for this pain to go away.
you can change your life
and all that makes you unhappy.
you can take your life into your own hands
without killing or hurting yourself.
-stay, V.

I think back to my 11-year-old self
the little mind who didn't
want to fight her own mind anymore.
the little mind who felt that one day
she would go crazy enough
to end it all.
but look,
i'm still here 15 years later,
loving life.
and you,
will love life too,
but,
you have to stay
to get there too,
and you will get there.
-please stay, VI.

I don't love myself
i've come to realize.
i cut myself no slack
and am quick to point out my flaws.
i'm not proud of who I am
and I feel as if I've wasted too much time,
with excuses and laziness.
but this self-hate ends here
and right now,
-It has to.

My heart aches at the young girl
whose fragile heart
has been broken by a boy
she thought loved her.
-it's okay to stay a virgin.

I shed tears at those whose bodies
were shot at by men
who saw their childlike physique
and made a war zone
out of their innocence.

So much pain in this world
could be solved if parents
truly understood the deep
and true importance
of a healthy home.
-the home is one of the roots of all evil.

I watch person after person
walk the same broken streets
with the same crumbled insides
with the same shattered mind
and bruised and scarred hearts.
if this is you, which I know it is,
because it is me too,
it's time to heal.

Brokenness is the new black.
-it's okay to be broken.

It's okay to be broken
because now you can learn
what it truly feels like to be whole.

The universe is comprised of things.
but,
God, created them all.
praise Him for all that happenings in your life,
for...
why thank an item,
when you can thank its Creator.

The eyes I carry now
are the same eyes I
carried as a child.
they saw too much
and maybe not enough.
they saw her parents
hold hands for the first time at age 14,
and the next day they saw her mother's lips
mouth they are getting divorced.
-these eyes, I.

These eyes saw porn at age eight.
-these eyes, II.

These eyes envision stories
of her mother underneath the fists of men
who taught her she was nothing.
these eyes also saw her mother
become superwoman.
-these eyes, III.

These eyes saw alcohol
turn her dad into a monster.
these eyes saw his eyes glow
a deep red.
these eyes saw when his demons
came out to play.
but these eyes have also seen
her dad sober.
and these eyes have seen
her dad turn into one of her favorite people.
-these eyes, IV.

These eyes know
what it feels like to cry
and to burn
they are not newcomers to pain,
they are experts.
-these eyes, V.

These eyes have witnessed
blood on wrists that
weren't hers
these eyes have witnessed
silence
and noise
that made her shake under her
mommy's robe.
-these eyes, VI.

These eyes have also
seen love and joy.
they have witnessed
smiles and laughter
and kisses and hugs.
these eyes have seen
peace and Heaven on earth.
-these eyes, VII.

I'm not going to tell you
it will always be a happy ending.
because many times
unhappy "endings" must occur before
true happiness can arise.
but, stay,
wait for your happiness to reveal itself—
it will come.
it always does.
-stay, VII.

They say your body holds onto everything,
that it forgets not.
which is why so many
people live with pain.
but, I'm beginning to understand
it's not just your body that
forgets not.
it's also:
-your heart
-your mind
-your eyes
-your ears
-your nose
-and your mouth
which is why triggers come in all sort of ways.
it's time to press the reset button
and let it go.

I'm glad I'm broken right now
because when I become full,
and whole once again,
i will appreciate it more
and the few scars that will remain.
-it's okay to have some scars.

You are broken,
and you know what?
-that's okay.

I have entered homes where the silent unhappiness
is ever present
where late night fights still resides in the walls
and where lingering arguments
echo through the emptiness in every room
where tears have stained the pillows
and the bathroom reeks of stale blood and vomit
i have entered homes where the floors creek with
unforgiveness
and the carpets hide away all secrets
these are the homes where cries aren't heard
and sadness is not seen outside its walls.
-these homes are right in front of you, yet we don't
see them
or at least we choose not to.
But I see them.

Leave the pills on the nightstand
and the alcohol in the fridge
keep the knife in the drawer
and the rope in the basement
put the razor blade back where you found it
and put the gun back in the closet
you're not ending tonight
this chapter still has pages left to write
your book doesn't end here…
-stay, VIII.

He knew his god and he had to have it
his hands constantly fondled the body of her
and his mind forever fantasized about when
he could get his hands on her again.
he lusted after an exotic French girl
and he obsessed over the way she made him feel;
for, no other woman made him feel like she did.
every day he struggled to stay faithful
and every day he failed.
he couldn't bear the thought of not having her
so he never denied himself of her.
Pinto Grigio was a lucky woman
she saw the most vulnerable sides
of my dad.
she had my dad's heart
and we all knew—
he wouldn't come back home to us
until he indulged in her fully,
not until he had his fix and slept the night away.
he wouldn't come back home to us
because they were a match made in hell.

I sit quiescently
and watch the radiant scintilla
of the mellifluous lullaby
of the waters flow.
the plethora of sapphire
hues in the somnolent moonlight
is like a symphony of
bliss and tranquility
in my zenith of serenity.
i sit remembering the halcyon
moments of my day
with admiration to its Creator.

Alcohol is the evil of the morning
the demon in the daytime
and the devil at night.
and you were its playground

Whispers in the dark fill my mind
screams at me during the day
and take residency in my head.
it's a constant battle between
self and I
a never ending fight
between common sense
and fight or flight
anxiety is an ongoing war
white flags raised
won't stop it from charging towards you
-anxiety, III.

she watched alcohol turn her father into a monster
she watched how the anger began to slowly take over
his body,
possessing him into something out of her nightmares
she couldn't run from his attacks
she couldn't break free from his grip
because she never knew when his monster would
possess,
until it's too late.

She remembers how his breath smelled
and how his shoes sounded on the floor
she can still see his eyes reddened with
anger and she can still feel how the house
shook when the monster within awoke
from its daily slumber.
she can place herself back in her room
and relive all those nights
when she feared for her
mother.

She doesn't drink
and she accredits that to her dad.
she sees what destruction
it caused to her father
and she tells people
that's why her lips have never
and will never
taste any drop of alcohol.
but that's not the reason.
honestly,
she wouldn't mind drinking.
her real reason is God.
and if it wasn't for Him
she would have be just like her father used to be…
but worse.
God is the reason why she is sober writing these
words.

I know these thoughts terrify you
but this episode will soon pass.
do me a favor and listen to my voice
and not the one whispering to you now.
stand to your feet and breathe in deep.
allow oxygen to get into your lungs
and let it transfer to every part of your body.
your heart.
your brain.
these thoughts are scary
trust me I know the fear.
i know the pain.
but God doesn't give us more than we can't handle
so I know you can get through this moment
and all to come.
keep fighting
you're doing great
because you're not leaving me tonight.
-stay, IX.

Don't pick up that gun
or swallow that pill
leave the old rusty razor blade
on the table
tomorrow needs to see you
tomorrow needs to hear your voice
and see your eyes and smile
tomorrow needs to feel your presence
in this world.
i need to see you tomorrow
and hear your laughter
and feel your presence
i need to see you rise above
the monster attacking you right now.
-stay, X.

I need to see your lungs full of air
and full of life tomorrow
don't leave me tonight
don't leave me at all
because I will notice
your absence.
-stay, XI.

You don't need someone to tell you
that they know how you feel
because you already know they don't.
you don't need someone to try and convince you not
to do it
because in your head your mind may already be made
up
you need someone to listen
listen to understand
you need someone to hear your
whispers in the dark
your cries for help.
you're not screaming loud
but you're loud enough
it's our fault for not listening,
for not taking the time to listen for the
whispers in the dark.
which is sad…
because the dark is the easiest place
to hear the softest sound.
-don't give up. Keep pushing through, your screams
will be heard. Never stop seeking help.
i hear you.
-stay, XII.

You scream to yourself
in the loneliness of the silent night
when moon cascades your bedroom
and star light decorates the blackened sky.
you lay alone in an oversized bed
wrapped in a blanket
with tears finding their way down your cheeks
with puffy eyes
and a sore throat
you fall asleep
with the hope that tomorrow is a new day.
you want all the pain to be done
and you want a smile to make its way back to your
face
don't worry love,
laughter will soon
find its home
back in your heart.

Keep fighting
keep hoping
keep your heart beating,
beating another day.
please don't leave me tonight.
-stay, XIII.

These words serve as a therapy session
for my mind and my heart
all the issues I thought I've dealt with
always seem to find their way back
when a pen is braced between my fingers
so I let out all my forgotten pain
and all my worries
here on these pages
so please handle with care
this is a therapy session after all.

I opened the door to fear years ago
he came in, settled down and is now my shadow
i've tried to kick him out
but the more I fight the more I doubt
if I can survive without him by my side
since he's been along for the ride
for so long now
i feel like I can't function without it,
i won't know how
for fear finds every chance to take a peak
and seek his moment to make me weak.
so I keep him locked inside my mind
because if I open the door
i know that before he leaves
he will cause a war.
but I guess he might have the power to control me
behind closed doors.
since I won't unlock his door
and release his final roar.
-avoiding problems, I.

Fear is a rolling thunder
and I count its seconds after the lightning
to see how close it is to me.
with each lighting strike
it creeps up closer to me
until I'm standing underneath it's roar
and it paralyzes me into submission.
-anxiety, IV.

I get stuck in these moods
where I lose all motivation
where I'd prefer to lay in bed all day
and watch time tick away.
it's like I'm a melting iceberg in the arctic
and the ever warming sun
is slowly melting me away
as I sit there frozen and watch it happen.

The water runs down the river
and she watches her pain ride it's waves
she watches it hit the rocks
and plummet down the fall
she watches it bounce around in the rapids
and as the current takes it away.
it is a long journey till it reaches its destination
whether it be a large body of water to get lost in
or to the ground will it will dry up and be gone
forever
she has surrendered her pain
at the head of the river
and like Moses's mom
prays it gets into the right hands.
                    God's.

She sat still.
unable to move,
or breathe
or speak.
you undressed her with your eyes
and then with your hands.
unaware, or choosing to ignore
the paralyzed look in her eyes,
that she doesn't want you.
yet, you continued,
heedless of the pain you will inflict upon her body
and her heart.
and all the lasting trauma that will take her years to
unfold.
she wants to forget
to move on
and keep it behind her.
but the constant terror she feels
when she closes her eyes at night
reminds her of why she can't forget.
for fear is not something that can go away when eyes
shut.
for fear, is conquered when faced head on.

It's so easy to give up on yourself.
to not want to try any longer.
people tell you, you are worthless
that you are meaningless.
they tell you, you are better off dead.
that you will amount to nothing.
but to those people,
i say…
just wait.

       please don't leave me tonight.
       -stay, XIV.

I know that you don't want to be here
that the word tomorrow paralyzes you
with emptiness and numbness.
i know that you'd rather end it right now
so that you don't have to wake to see tomorrow.
but tomorrow isn't today
and it isn't yesterday either.
it's not two days from now
and it's not a week from today.
or a year.
tomorrow is tomorrow
a new day
a day you haven't even lived yet.
it's a new start you haven't given a change to yet.
it's a place and a time that you,
yes you—
need to be in.
because tomorrow isn't so scary when it's here.
it's today that makes tomorrow look so frightening.
and tomorrow will be better than today;
because you will have lived another day.
and you will conquer the voices in your head,
saying that tomorrow doesn't need you.
when in reality,
every day past, present, and future;
needs you.
-stay, XV.

Nakedness does not show the power of women.

Young girls are learning to be sexy,
before they even understand what being sexy means.
-protect our girls

Little girls are being taught that
their minds and the knowledge that they uphold
has far less value than their bodies.

Used, and abused
you hold onto pain
like its keeping you alive.
-it's killing you.

Today may have been tough,
but tonight you need to get some sleep.
stop worrying, and don't fret.
leave it all to God to take care of.
now shut your eyes, and rest.
tomorrow is a new day.

There comes a point in life
when you can't blame your mom or your dad
for the way you act.

My mind is really good at
convincing myself of things
i know are not true.

If you go into the Bible
with preconceived notions,
then all you will see
are those preconceptions.

Anxiety ate are her in the middle of the night
and suffocated her throughout the day.
a constant battle between
sanity and insanity.
-anxiety, V.

But when she cried
everyone else used
their own unhappiness
to drown out her cries for help.

In a world full of fear and destruction,
be someone's peace and joy.

These thoughts make me feel
like I am drowning in the ocean,
constantly fighting the waves,
trying to keep my head above the water.
but the harder I try to stay afloat,
the deeper I sink.
-anxiety, VI.

I hate that you still make me mad.
        -to everyone that hurt me.

You were down by the shore
        collecting shells for your collection.
one by one
you gathered ones that looked perfect to you.
        avoiding the ones with cracks and holes.
you wanted the ones that were not abused
        by the waves
you wanted the ones that you wished you could be.
        perfect.
        beautiful.
but little did you know that the scarred and broken
ones
        were just as beautiful,
and even with the abuse
        they still glisten with beauty
under the moonlight and the sun.

God turns worthlessness
into the most valuable.

I wonder what it would be like,
if all children were heard.

Before there are mistakes,
there are decisions.

But the silence of the night,
always seems to be the
loudest to me.

We must teach our young girls
that their bodies are worth more
than sex, and that their minds are worth
more than their bodies.

But, here I am writing,
trying to put the pieces of myself
together again,
within the skeletons of these poems.

She stares down at the blank floor
where she remembers foot steps
and those footsteps remember trauma
trauma is such a strong word
but it feels right rolling off her tongue
as if her insides rolled right out with
its utterance,
and onto the floor
where trauma hit.
she hates it here
she hates it in this skin she can't shed
but she fights to live
because she knows the grave
only welcomes the dead,
and she truly isn't ready to die.
-you will get through this
-stay, XVI.

My mirror broke
cracks remain in the glass
yet it never shattered.
just like you have been broken
yet you remain standing and still work.
you may feel shattered
but you're not.
you can still breathe
you can still feel
you are not shattered
you are bruised and carry scars
but you can still live through it all—
because bruises will fade
and many scars will be forgotten in due time.
you just,
kcep living.

She pulls down black sleeves
to hide dried blood
that she never wiped away.
this one crusted over
next to the one that has healed.
she is tip toeing around suicide
and I ask you now,
to please place the blade down
step away
and leave that space.
demons are talking to you
but ignore them
and hear these words…
you will be missed
and you are loved by people
you don't think do.
please don't leave me tonight.
-stay, XVII.

She wonders why pain stays inside her
like a sickness that poisons blood
and penetrates bone
and lives in marrow.
she can't rid herself of pain
no matter how much she vomits.
blood transfusions only make it worse
and medicine only coats the hurt.
but my love,
maybe it's time to face the pain
and let it run away from the new you,
in fear.
-avoiding problems, II.

She woke up in a bed,
not her bed.
a stranger in a strangers bed.
she's naked
from the inside, out.
vulnerable
and crushed under a weight
that presses down on her heart.
she feels her pulse in her head
and she's gonna be sick
not from the alcohol from last night
but at the thought of allowing someone
to enter her sanctuary
without her knowledge.
-stay in tonight, don't go home with him, V.

He always had a wine glass
in his hand
or I could always count on it
being close by.
whenever my dad couldn't show up
i knew the glass would make
and appearance.

I don't drink
and not because I never wanted to
i don't drink
because I saw how demons hide
at the bottom of bottles
and show their face
in the eyes of its victim.
-intoxicated people make me nervous

I entered the sexual entrapment
at the age of eight.
-porn destroys

I sometimes feel like my mind
is not my own,
and that these thoughts
don't belong to me.
-anxiety, VII.

Many people love you
and all the many talents
they say you can do.
but, to be honest with you,
i can't stand you.
the sight of you terrifies me
and when you become a part of a person,
anxiety rushes through me.
just like when I see your cousin,
alcohol.
-high people make me nervous.

She moves at night and with the waves
she drifts to new places
and always has the same intentions
of staying awhile,
but the tide calls her to move on
she has trouble committing
and remaining faithful
but it may be because
of all those who should have
committed to her
yet rolled back into the ocean.
they taught her
to ride the waves
instead of staying ashore.
-a girl who never had a dad.

Tears glisten in her eyes
but he mistakes them for stars
blinded by her beauty
he forgot to notice her pain.
her body held onto moonlight
but he failed to see her scars reflecting
he didn't even realize
that he cut her deeply
before leaving her
like the rest.
-don't go home with him, VI.

Just because time has gone by
doesn't mean all wounds have been healed.
it's going to hurt for a while,
and cuts will constantly be reopened.
but hear me when I say,
it will get better
&
you'll be okay

Don't go.

Please stay.

You are loved more than you think.
you think you aren't,
but think again.
-I love you.

Since when has the moon
not shone at night?
i search for a light to guide
me home,
but I'm stuck in darkness
roaming the streets
hoping to land at my doorstep
before morning breaks.
-lost in my thoughts

My mind has captured me
and taken me under arrest.
i am a prisoner
ready to break free.
but these tired hands
are weak
but this backbone
won't let me sink
into the deep chambers
of this circle dome of a mind.
because,
i can
escape
and I will lock the doors behind me.

You will be missed.
-don't believe those thoughts.

I am not yet a mother
so I can't yet understand
that love.
but, based on my mother
i can tell its
out of this world.

Scarlet water falls from your wrist
next to dormant scars
laid out like a perfectly lined list.
please,
put the blade down
and understand one thing for me:
         you don't need to do this
stick around to find out the many reasons
God created you.
you have a purpose.
-stay, XVIII.

There is only one of you,
so make it count.

I sit under the willow tree
and think.
i think about how different
my life could be
if i'd actually
do something
i've only spoke about.
if i'd actually do
something
i've only dreamt about.

Sometimes it's okay to cry
like a baby.
for babies hold nothing back.
they allow themselves to feel
and they release it all
and then they are happy
but,
we have been,
taught by indoctrination
that to cry means to be
vulnerable
and vulnerability leads to pain
so we fight back tears.
but, I think it's time for you to
cry,
like a baby.
-hold nothing back.

You hold the gun in
your hands
and the power you feel
rushes through your
blood.
you want to hurt
people
and you probably don't
know why.
their lives lay at the
end of the barrel
you're holding
and this gives you life,
if only for a moment.
you open fire,
and pull triggers
but you really only
want
someone to pull you in
to their arms
and snatch the gun
away.
you want to feel heard
and you want to be
noticed.
the thoughts that enter
your mind
scare you,

and you're not
yourself.
you've planned this,
but it's not too late to
stop.
i think you just
want someone to else
to feel fear
and to feel death
tickling the back of
their neck
like you do, every day.
you feel alone,
your subtle ways of
crying out
were never heard
and I'm sure home
felt more like hell.
but, my love,
it doesn't need to end
this way.
you don't need to take
someone's life,
and you don't need to
take yours.
there is always
someone who
wants to listen.

there is always
someone who,
cares…
you just have to give
someone a chance
and that someone can
be me.

before you pull the
trigger,
call me.
put the gun down,
and I will listen,
wherever you are.
-to a gunman I.

You are staring down
the end of a barrel
flirting with your life,
and others.
you want the thoughts
to stop
you want the pain to
end.
too many late nights
talking to darkness
has brought you here,
and you see no other
way.
the ones you're going
after
have probably hurt you
ignored you
annoyed you
and you can't stand
them.
i get the pain
but it can't end like
this.
you may have a gun,
but their life is not in
your hands,
and neither is yours.
what happens after?

when they sleep in
graves
and mothers weep in
pain
after their child who
slept
within them are no
longer
breathing?
no longer living this
life they helped to
create?
this is much bigger
than you.
i know your heart
aches
it is shattered.
you want someone to
miss you
like those mothers will
miss their
sleeping child.
so hear me when I say
this:
you would be missed
deeper
than you want to
believe.
your missing voice

your vacant smile
your silent laugh
will be recognized…
and missed at your
forever absence.
whether you're
planning to
take your life
or live behind bars
for taking someone
else's,
you would be deeply
missed.
so, please,
put the gun away and
run to help.

think of one person
you know,
who can help.
no matter how strange
and random
they may be,
run into their arms
for help
because your life
matters,
&
their lives matter
and it does not
and cannot
end like this.

-to a gunman, II.

He is a storm
destruction lies beneath his eyes
and pain hides under
his heart.
darkness flows within his body
and blocks out light.
the storm is boiling
ready to take action
to break the calmness of
the surface.
But something is
parting the black smog that layers
the opening and
light streams in,
warming up the coldness
in his heart.
the light has filtered out
all the darkness
and he rises
with new life
a new lightness
and that light
is a result
of calling God.
The Ultimate Storm Calmer,
The Ultimate
Healer.

These thoughts
they talk to you.
they reside in your nightmares,
and come out to play
during the day.
they grab your hand
and lead you down
& into
a path of darkness.
they want you to get lost
among the blackened light
so they let go of your hand
and run away.
leaving you,
in the darkened
labyrinth of your own mind.

Don't leave your sorrows at the bottom of bottles,
or at the emptiness of pill containers.
don't leave your pain
at the feet of man
and expect your scars to be healed.
don't allow your hurts
to reside at the end of razor blades
that sit on your bed side.
don't let your fears
and your thoughts of being worthless
take rest at the end of a barrel.
the pain may be here today
but one moment,
one morning
you will wake
and you will realize
that you can face the day.
please live to face today
please live to face the tomorrows
to come.
because the pain won't last
through all
tomorrows to come.
-stay, XIX.

Your body is squeezed tight.
as if you can't get oxygen
back into your lungs.
you're in the midst of an attack
with fists clenched
and eyes squeezed tight
you can't see
or hear anything
besides the thoughts
that take place behind your shut eyes.
your nails have dug into your skin
and your chest feels as if a snake
has wrapped its body around you
and squeezed
and squeezed
and squeezed
so tight
that you can barely breathe.
you fight against an enemy
that pretends to be there.
but yet,
you still have battle wounds
from a fictious
enemy,
a pretend
war.
-anxiety, VIII.

You stare down at your feet
wondering why they won't move.
wondering why you can't take steps.
right then left, right then left,
and get yourself out.
you look down at your feet and
wonder why they are stuck
in the place you now reside.
you want to leave,
but, your body rebels.
your mind is telling you to go,
but your heart has told you to stay.
you look down at your feet,
and wonder why you're still here
why you're still there.
however,
the answer doesn't reside in your feet,
but in the seriousness and dictation
from your mind.
-control your thoughts, control yourself.
        -don't give your body any options-

There is a difference
between love and desire.
love is not merely just a feeling
and desire is fueled by emotions—
most of the time,
temporary emotions.
-love is a commitment.

You have been through hell
you have been hurt & abused
and you've had enough
i'm here to tell you that
you are strong.
you can and you will overcome this.

You think it won't get better,
but the sun always comes after
the darkest nights.

When it comes to my mind
i wonder if anyone would understand.
but then there are people like you,
reading this book,
and I know I'm not alone.

Your childlike innocence still resides
within your heart,
even though many things were
snatched from you
at such a young age.
find that innocence again.

Allow these words
this book
to remind you that
you are not alone in
this war against your mind.
-anxiety, IX.

There will be a day
and soon
when you look back
and realize
you had the strength all along.

You are not a piece of garbage
you are royalty.
you've made mistakes
and people have used you,
but you are just as much royalty
as the next person.
we are all children of a King.

You have done things you're not proud of,
you were forced to do.
you were under the control
of a man who exploited you.
but my love,
you are beautiful
and you are loved.
you are not worthless.
-to a woman who was sex trafficked

I know you feel alone.
i know you feel as if you have no one.
but don't allow those demons to speak to you.
they are infamous liars.

Leave those drugs in their hiding spot tonight.
don't take them out.
embrace the night,
embrace your feelings.
call someone to talk to
cry out.
i'm listening.

Just because you used to do it
doesn't mean you have to do it
now.
leave it in the past.
even if the past begins right now.
you can do it.
you can do anything you put your mind to.
let's begin right now.

I can't wait to hear your stories of victory.
-share them with me.

You've had a lot of people give up on you.
but there are three things I need you to remember.

I.   You can never give up on yourself.
II. I will never give up on you
III. God can never and will never give up on you.

Down at the end of the long river
lies a woman
her hair parted slightly to the side,
and her eyes wet.
her nose small,
and her mouth partly open.
her feet are in the sand,
and her head tilted back
looking up into the moving clouds
saturated with black birds.
she imagines flying away,
but she chooses to stay.
she imagines,
her life.
And
She is ready to concur hers.
-she has found her purpose in this life.

-Stay.
XX.

To my readers,

I want you to know that it is okay to get help with whatever you are dealing with. There are so many people in this world who have good hearts, and want to help. I have listed below the suicide hotline, where you can call anytime, and they can help get you through those dark episodes.

National Suicide Prevention Lifeline:
1-800-273-8255

Prayer has helped me in my lowest moments, and I know God will listen to your words and all you say to Him. Give prayer a chance. I have written one you can speak below:

God you know these thoughts in my head, you know the very things in which I am struggling with. Please quiet my mind, and allow me to hear your voice, and feel your peace within me. Wrap your arms around me and all others in this moment, and help me to trust you are in control, and that I will be okay.
In Jesus name, amen.

God hears, and He will answer. Patience is key. God's timing is perfect.

Proverbs 3:5-6
"Trust in the Lord with all your heart, and lean not on your own understanding. Seek His will in all you do, and He will show you which path to take."

You are loved, you are needed in this world, and you have a purpose.

Follow me on Instagram:
@m.blackmore

Check out my website as well:
www.meganblackmore.com

About the author:
Megan Blackmore was born on November 22, 1994, and is married to her husband Francesco Blackmore, her "high school sweetheart. "She loves living in Connecticut, and she graduated from Central Connecticut State University with a degree in English and Writing in 2018. She has always loved to write, and she always remembers having a notebook or a drawing pad in hand. Writing and art were her first forms of therapy, and poetry has taken over her heart in the arts world.

Thank you all for reading!
-M.Blackmore

Printed in Great Britain
by Amazon

59157164R00102